CONTENTS

CHILDREN'S BIBLE STORIES

From the New Testament

Retold by **Nancy Martin**

Illustrated by **Gwen Green**

Ideals Publishing Corp.
Milwaukee, Wisconsin

Jesus Is Born

A long time ago, when the Romans were powerful, the Governor wanted to find out how many of his subjects were living in his country. He ordered them all to leave their homes and go to the place where their fathers and mothers and grandparents had lived.

Joseph and Mary lived in Nazareth, and Mary was pledged to marry Joseph. They had to travel seventy miles south to Bethlehem, and the journey took a long time.

When Mary and Joseph arrived, the town was full of people. The first thing Joseph did was to look for a place where they could sleep but all he could find was a stable. He wished he could have found somewhere more comfortable because he knew Mary was expecting her baby to be born very soon. He also knew this was going to be an extra special baby, because God had told him so.

That very night the baby was born and they called him Jesus. That was the very first Christmas Day.

This happened nearly two thousand years ago and people all over the world still remember Christmas Day as the birthday of Jesus.

Wise Men Worship Jesus

When a new baby is born the news quickly spreads. Although there were no newspapers, radio or television, some wise men had been looking at the stars and waiting for the news. When they saw a special star they decided to go and see King Herod in Jerusalem.

'Where is the baby who is to be King of the Jews?' they asked. 'We saw his star in the east and have come to worship him.'

Herod was very worried. He did not want anyone to take his place as king. He called all the priests and teachers together and asked where this new baby would be found.

'In Bethlehem, in Judea,' they replied. 'That is where the prophets said he would come from.'

Herod turned to the wise men.

'Go to Bethlehem and search for this baby. When you find him come and tell me so that I can go and worship him.'

He did not want to worship Jesus. He only wanted to get rid of him.

The wise men went and the star they had seen in the east stopped right over the place where Jesus was born.

The men were very happy when they saw Jesus lying in the manger. They bowed down and worshipped him. Then they gave him the presents they had brought. But they did not go back to Herod because they had a dream which told them to go home another way.

Listening and Questioning

Mary and Joseph went to the Feast of the Passover in Jerusalem with their relatives and friends. Jesus went too.

Jesus was only twelve but he spent most of the time in the temple listening to the teachers and asking questions.

When it was time to go his parents thought he was with their friends. When a day passed and he was not with them, they decided to return to Jerusalem.

And there they found him. He was still in the temple with the teachers.

His mother was very surprised to see him there. He did not seem a bit bothered at being left behind.

'Son,' said Mary, 'why have you treated us like this? Your father and I have been anxiously searching for you.'

'Why were you searching for me?' asked Jesus. 'Didn't you know I had to be in my Father's house?'

His parents did not know what he was talking about, but his mother thought about all the things Jesus said and did.

Jesus Is Baptised

As Jesus grew older he heard a lot about a man who was called John the Baptist.

One day Jesus asked John to baptise him. But John hesitated. He knew Jesus was a very special person, so he said:

'I need to be baptised by you. It is not for me to baptise you.'

But Jesus insisted.

'It is right for you to do this for me,' he said. 'It is what God wants.'

Then Jesus walked into the water and John baptised him. As Jesus came out he heard a voice saying:

'This is my Son, whom I love, and I am very pleased with him.'

9

Tempted to Do Wrong

Jesus was nearly thirty years old. It would soon be time for him to start his special work for God, so he went to a quiet place to think and pray about it.

He was there such a long time that he began to feel hungry. If only the stones he could see around him were bread.

'If you are the Son of God tell these stones to become bread,' said a little voice.

Jesus knew he was the Son of God. He knew he was going to do wonderful things for him. Jesus knew that God was with him, but he also knew that the powers God had given him were to be used for his Father's glory and Kingdom, and not for his own needs or fame. So he answered:

'Man does not live by bread alone.'

And he walked away and climbed up to a high place. As he looked around he seemed to see all the kingdoms of the world. Again he heard the voice of the tempter:

'You can have all this for yourself if you want it. You can be powerful and great. You can become the most important man in the world.'

But once more Jesus knew that was not what God wanted for him. If he yielded to that temptation he would not be fulfilling God's purpose for him.

'It is written,' said Jesus firmly, 'worship the Lord your God and serve him only.'

Again Jesus went away from the temptation. But the tempter was not going to give up too easily.

'If you are the Son of God, climb to the highest point in the temple in Jerusalem and throw yourself down. You wouldn't be hurt.

God's angels would look after you. Try it.'

But Jesus was not going to yield to temptation. He knew all things were possible with God, but this was not his way for Jesus.

Now Jesus was really sure what God wanted him to do and he was ready to do it. He was going God's way.

The rest of the stories in this book show how he started working in God's way and went that way right to the very end of his life on earth.

The Marvellous Catch of Fish

When Jesus had faced his temptations and overcome them he started the work God had sent him to do. He began to choose men to be with him so that they might learn the way of the Kingdom of God.

One day, when he was walking by the Sea of Galilee, he saw some fishermen washing their nets. One of them was Simon, who was later known as Peter.

There was a crowd of people around Jesus so he got into Simon's boat and asked him to pull away from the shore. Simon did so and Jesus sat in the boat with Simon and the others and taught the people who were standing beside the water. When he had finished speaking he said to Simon:

'Pull out into deeper water and let down your fishing nets.'

'Master,' said Simon, 'it's no use. We've been fishing all night, and we've caught nothing. But if you say so we'll try again.'

Then they did as Jesus told them and soon their nets were so full of fish that they began to break. And the boat was so heavy with fish that it nearly sank.

The fishermen were astonished at the big catch of fish, and Simon was a little frightened. But Jesus said to him:

'Don't be afraid, Simon. From now on you will catch men.'

And Simon and the others knew that Jesus was calling them to be his disciples, so they left their nets and their fishing and followed Jesus.

13

Guest at a Wedding

One day Jesus and his mother were invited to a wedding. Part way through the wedding feast Mary heard that all the wine had been served. Mary always had known that Jesus was no ordinary son, so she went to him and said quietly:

'They have no more wine.'

'Why do you come to me about this?' asked Jesus.

Mary may have been surprised at the answer she got from Jesus, but she had great faith in him. She did not give up. Instead she went to the servants and simply said to them:

'Do whatever Jesus tells you to do.'

Standing near were six big stone water jars. The servants must have been surprised when Jesus told them to fill each one with water. They must have been even more surprised when Jesus said:

'Now draw some out and take it to the master of the banquet.'

But they did as he asked and took it to their master. When he had tasted it he did not ask the servants why they were serving water instead of wine. He called the bridegroom to him and said:

'Everyone brings out the choice wine first and then the cheapest, but you have saved the best till last.'

But the servants knew that Jesus must have performed a miracle and turned the water into wine.

Although Jesus would not perform a miracle and turn the stones into bread to satisfy his own hunger, he was willing and able to do this to make the wedding feast a happy occasion. And his mother's faith in him was rewarded.

The Man Who Could Not Walk

Four men had a friend who could not walk. All day he lay on his mat saying:

'If only I could go and see Jesus. I'm sure he would help me.'

'We must do something to help him,' one of his friends said one day.

'Let's carry him to Jesus,' said another. 'He has healed all sorts of people.'

So they each took a corner of the mat and carried him just as he was. When they got to the house where Jesus was teaching, the room was full of people. They were all around Jesus and the four men could not get near him. But they were determined to get their friend to Jesus somehow.

'We'll climb up on to the roof,' they said, 'and get him there that way.'

They were quite sure Jesus would make him walk again.

Once they were on the roof it was easy. They moved some of the tiles and lowered their friend through the hole they had made, until he lay on his mat right in front of Jesus.

Jesus looked at the man staring up at him so hopefully, but he did not tell him to get up. He surprised them all when he said:

'Friend, your sins are forgiven.'

Jesus knew what some of the teachers were thinking. They thought he was wrong to say this. Only God could forgive sins and they would not admit that Jesus was God.

'Why are you thinking these things?' asked Jesus. 'Which do you think is easier to say, "Your sins are forgiven," or "Get up and walk"?' Then he said to the man who could not walk:

'Get up, take your mat, and go home.'

Immediately the man stood up, took up his mat and went home, praising God.

Jesus said to the people around him:

'Now perhaps you will know that the Son of Man has power to forgive sins.'

All the people were amazed and filled with wonder.

'We have seen remarkable things today,' they said.

The Sower and the Seed

One of the reasons why people liked listening to Jesus was because he nearly always told them a story. It was usually about something the people were familiar with. Several of these stories, or parables, are in this book. Here is one of them.

A farmer went out to sow his seeds hoping for a good harvest. He walked up and down his land, scattering the seeds so that they could work their own way into the earth. But they did not always fall in the best places.

Some fell on the path, which was hard, so the seeds stayed on top and could not grow. Other seeds fell on dry, rocky ground, where there was not much moisture. Although little plants did start coming up their leaves began to wither and die for lack of water.

Some seeds fell among thorns. The thorny plants grew big and strong. They spread so quickly that the little seedlings were choked by the thorn bushes before they could grow into big strong plants.

The rest of the seeds fell in good soil. They went right into the earth and this helped them to grow well. When harvest time came there was a very good crop.

'What does this parable mean?' asked the disciples.

'The seed is God's word,' Jesus explained. 'That which fell on the path is like those people who hear God's message but do not understand what it means. What they hear doesn't sink into their hearts and minds.

'That which was sown in rocky places,' Jesus went on, 'is like those who hear and understand but as soon as something goes wrong they turn away from God. The message has not gone deep enough into their hearts.'

'What about the seed that fell among the thorns?' asked the disciples. 'What does that mean?'

'Those are the people who are so busy thinking about themselves and how they can make more money that there isn't room for God and he gets choked out of their lives. But the plants which grow on the good ground are those who hear and understand the message and let it grow strong in their hearts and minds.'

Stilling the Storm

Sometimes Jesus taught his disciples by telling them parables, as he did in the last story, and at other times they learned something from his miracles.

'Let's go over to the other side of the lake,' said Jesus one day.

It was quiet and peaceful in the boat and as Jesus was tired he soon fell asleep. While he slept a storm blew up. The wind lashed the waves against the boat until it started to fill with water. As they rocked about on the waves the disciples began to be afraid and wondered whether they ought to wake Jesus. They were used to storms but this was a really bad one and it was getting worse. They were afraid they would all be drowned.

At last they woke Jesus.

'Master, Master,' they called, 'wake up! We're going to be drowned.'

Jesus woke up. When he saw the storm he was not afraid. Very calmly he stood up.

'Peace be still,' he said.

His voice was calm and quiet and the disciples gazed in wonder as they felt the wind cease and saw the water grow placid and smooth.

Quietly Jesus turned to his disciples:

'Where is your faith?' he asked.

The disciples were too amazed to answer him, but as they drew the boat to shore and followed him they said to each other:

'Who is this that he commands even the waves and they obey him?'

They were to see many more wonderful things as they continued to follow him.

Feeding the Five Thousand

One day Jesus went to a quiet little town called
Bethsaida. He went there to be alone with his disciples
but the people soon found out where he was and they
followed him. They wanted to know more about him.

All through the day Jesus spoke to them and healed
the sick. Late in the afternoon the crowd was just as
big. The disciples were beginning to get hungry, so
they went to Jesus and said:

'Send the people away so they can go and find
food.' But Jesus said:

'You give them some.'

'We've only got five loaves of bread and two fishes,'
they replied. 'Do you want us to go and buy food for
all these people?'

There were about five thousand people so it was not
surprising that the disciples were astonished when
Jesus said, so calmly, 'You give them some food.'

Then Jesus said:

'Make them sit down in groups of about fifty each.'

When all were seated Jesus gave God thanks for the food and the disciples took it to the people.

There was more than enough to go round!

When everyone had eaten, the disciples filled twelve baskets with the food which was left over.

Jesus worked a miracle when there was a need but did not work miracles to satisfy his own needs.

The Good Samaritan

People were always asking Jesus questions. Sometimes he told them a story so that they could answer their own questions. He did this one day when a lawyer said:

'In the Law it is written, ''Love your neighbour as yourself,'' but who is my neighbour?'

Jesus told him this story:

'A man was on his way to Jerusalem when he was attacked by robbers. They took all that he had and went off, leaving him lying there half dead.

'Soon after a priest came along the road and saw the man lying there. He did not stop to see if he could do anything to help. He just went by on the other side of the road.

'The next man who came along was a Levite. He knew a lot about the Law, but, like the priest, he did not stop to help. He looked at the injured man and went by on the other side of the road.

'Then a Samaritan came along on a donkey. The Samaritans and the Jews were not friendly with each other, yet as soon as he saw the Jewish man looking so ill and in need of help, he stopped. He cleaned and bandaged the man's wounds, then he lifted him on to the donkey and walked beside him until they came to an inn. They stayed there that night.

'The next morning the Samaritan had to leave, but before he went he gave the innkeeper some money and said:

' ''Look after my friend and when I come back I will pay you any extra you spend on him.'' '

Jesus turned to the lawyer and said:

'Which of these three men was a neighbour to the man who fell among robbers?'

'The one who had mercy on him,' said the lawyer.

'Go and do thou likewise,' said Jesus.

The Rich Fool

One day a man in the crowd listening to Jesus said:

'Teacher, come and tell my brother to share what he has with me.'

Jesus replied:

'I have not been sent to settle such things between you, but be careful you don't become selfish and greedy. I'll tell you a story about what happened to a man who was selfish.

'It was harvest time and a certain farmer stood looking at the richness of the harvest his land had yielded. It was the best he had ever seen and he was very pleased. He was so pleased he could think of nothing else. There was so much his barns could not store it.

' "I know what I'll do," he said at last. "I'll build bigger barns."

'And he rubbed his hands together thinking of all the wealth he had for himself. Then he set to work. He pulled down his old barns and built big new ones. When he had finished he looked at them and thought:

' ''I shall be a very rich man when these are all filled. I shall have enough to last me for years and years.''

'He worked very hard to get all the work finished in time and he was very tired when he went to bed.

'And that night he died. He never harvested the corn he had thought so much about.'

The Mustard Seed

Most of the people who followed Jesus liked to see him working miracles. They also liked listening to his stories. But when he talked about the Kingdom of God, his listeners were not sure what he meant. So he told them.

'It's like the seed of the mustard tree,' he said. 'The seed is very small but if you plant it in your garden it will grow and spread and become a fine big tree. Then the birds will come and sit on the branches.'

That's like the Kingdom of God. From small beginnings it will go on growing until it becomes really big.

One Sheep Is Lost

Some of the people who followed Jesus began to find fault with him. One of the things they said was:

'This man welcomes sinners and eats with them.'

Jesus heard what they said, so he told them another parable.

'If any of you had a hundred sheep and one was lost, you wouldn't stay with the ninety-nine who were safely in the fold. You would leave them and go and look for the lost one, and you would keep on looking until you found it. Then you would call your neighbours and say to them:

' ''Be glad with me because I have found my lost sheep.''

'That's how God feels. He is very happy when even one sinner says he is sorry and comes back to his fold.'

The Son Who Came Back

Jesus told many stories to show that God is very forgiving. One was about a man whose younger son wanted to have a good time, so one day he said to his father:

'Give me my share of your money so that I can go away.'

Once he got the money the son felt free—free to do as he liked. He had his good time, but soon his money was spent. He did not even have enough money left to buy food for himself, and he was hungry. Then he began to think of his father and the comfortable home he had left.

'Even the servants in my father's house are better off than I am,' he said. 'They will not be hungry, like me.'

And he wished he was home again.

'I'll go back,' he said, 'and when I see my father again I'll say, "Father, I have sinned against you and against God. I've spent all your money and I'm not worthy to be your son. Make me one of your hired men."'

Now the father had been looking for his son. He felt sure he would come back some time, and one day he saw him trudging wearily along the road towards home. His father was so glad that he ran to meet him.

'Father,' said the son, 'I have sinned against God and against you and I am not worthy to be called your son.'

He had no time to say the bit about making him a servant because his father threw his arms about him and kissed him, and took him straight back home.

'Go quickly,' he told the servants. 'Get the best robe you can find for my son. Put a ring on his finger, and sandals on his feet. And you others, you go and get a fatted calf and make a feast for us, for this son of mine was lost and is found. He has come back home.'

The Pharisee and the Tax Collector

Some of those in the crowd who followed Jesus thought they were good and had no need for forgiveness because they obeyed the law. They were proud people and thought themselves better than others. So Jesus told them a parable.

'A Pharisee and a Tax Collector went up to the temple to pray,' began Jesus. 'The Pharisee stood up to pray and said:

'"God, I thank you that I am not like other men. I don't do anything wrong. I don't rob or steal as other men do. I'm not like other men."

'He was a very proud man and very satisfied with himself.

'Then he saw the Tax Collector standing a little distance away with bowed head. He did not like Tax Collectors, so he added to his prayer.

'"I'm not like this Tax Collector. I fast twice a week and give away a tenth of all I have."

'But the Tax Collector was praying too, and his prayer was very different. He was a humble man and he simply said:

'"God have mercy on me, a sinner." '

Jesus liked people to be humble, but this man also knew he sometimes did things which were wrong. He knew he needed God's forgiveness.

Then Jesus said to the listening people:

'I tell you, this man, rather than the Pharisee, went home accepted by God.'

Jesus knew the Pharisee was not sorry for what he had done wrong.

33

34

The Leper Who Gave Thanks

When Jesus was living in Galilee there were a lot of people who had leprosy. It was one of the diseases that nobody really knew how to cure. Those who suffered with it had to keep away from other people because nobody wanted to catch it. So the lepers became poor and lonely.

One day, when Jesus was entering a village, ten men who had leprosy called to him in loud voices.

'Master, have pity on us.'

They did not come near Jesus—they just waited to see what he would do.

When Jesus saw them he simply said:

'Go, show yourselves to the priests.'

He said this because he knew that only the priests were allowed to say they could mix with other people again.

The men did as Jesus said. Although he had not touched them, or even said they were cured, they trusted him. And as they went they found the leprosy had gone.

One of the ten men turned back when he knew he was healed. The leper fell at the feet of Jesus and said:

'Thank you, Master, you have cured me of the leprosy.'

'Where are the others?' asked Jesus. 'Why has only one come to say thank you?'

Then he turned to the man and said:

'Rise up, and go your way. Your faith has made you well.'

Triumphal Entry Into Jerusalem

Although Jesus had his enemies he also had a lot of friends. When the time came for him to go to Jerusalem for the last time, he called two of his disciples to him and said:

'Go to the next village. When you get there you will find a colt tied. No one has yet ridden him. Untie him and bring him to me. If anyone wants to know why you are untying him, tell them the Lord needs him.'

The two disciples did as Jesus asked and they found the colt as he had said. They were untying him when the owners came by.

'Why are you untying the colt?' they asked.

The disciples of Jesus replied as Jesus had told them to do:

'The Lord needs him.'

When they had taken the colt to Jesus, they threw their cloaks over the animal and sat Jesus on him.

Then Jesus began his ride into Jerusalem. Crowds of people lined the way. They waved palms and laid their cloaks on the ground, so that Jesus could ride on them like the King he was. They were full of joy and called aloud their praise to God for all the miracles and wonderful things they had seen Jesus do.

'Blessed is the King who comes in the name of the Lord,' they chanted. 'Peace in heaven and glory in the highest.'

Although some of the Pharisees wanted Jesus to stop people from making so much noise and praising him, Jesus would not stop them. It really was a triumphal entry into Jerusalem for Jesus.

The Last Supper

It was time for the Feast of the Passover and Jesus wanted to go to this with his disciples. Just before it was time to set off he asked Peter and John to go to Jerusalem to prepare for the feast.

'As you enter the city,' he told them, 'a man carrying a jar of water will meet you. Follow him and go into the house where he goes. Ask the owner to show you the Guest Room where we can have the feast together. Tell him I have sent you. Then he will show you to an upper room where you can make the preparations.'

The disciples did as Jesus asked, and when the day came to go all was ready. Jesus gathered the disciples around him at the table. It was to be an occasion they would never forget.

'I have been looking forward to this supper for some time,' Jesus said, 'because it will be the last time I shall share a supper with you before I suffer.'

Then he took the passover bread and gave thanks before passing it round to each of the disciples. As he did so he said:

'This is my body, given for you. Do this in remembrance of me.'

They ate the bread and supper began. At the end Jesus took the wine in his hand and said:

'This is the new covenant in my blood, which is poured out for you. Drink it in remembrance of me.'

The disciples wondered at the meaning of it all, but they felt it was a very special occasion. This made it all the more surprising to them when Jesus said:

'One of you, sitting at this table, is going to betray me.'

We can imagine the questions the disciples must have asked themselves. Why should anyone who had been a disciple of Jesus do such a thing?

But they soon found out, because one of them did betray Jesus that very night.

His name was Judas—Judas Iscariot.

This last supper which Jesus had with his disciples was so special that it has become one of the church services. All those who love Jesus are invited to attend and take part in the service. The bread and wine are served to the people at this special service where Christians remember Christ's death and resurrection. It is a very important memorial service when Christians all over the world remember that last supper which Jesus had with his disciples.

Betrayal and Arrest

There were often times when Jesus wanted to go to a quiet place to pray. Sometimes he went to the Mount of Olives. He went there after warning the disciples that one of them would betray him.

The disciples went with him, but Jesus wanted to be alone with God. So he said to them:

'You stay here and pray that you are not tempted.'

Then he left them and went on a little way before he knelt down to pray. First he thought of what he knew was going to happen to him and he knew he would need God's help to bear it all.

'Father,' he said, 'if you are willing, take this suffering away from me. Yet not my will but yours be done.'

He felt stronger as he knew God had heard his prayer, but he went on praying. He knew he was going to have a very bad time, and he must be brave to bear it.

When he had finished praying he went back to the disciples. They were all asleep.

'Why are you sleeping?' he asked. 'Get up and pray so that you will be strong enough to overcome temptation.'

As he said this a crowd of men carrying swords and clubs came towards them. Leading them was Judas, one of the disciples of Jesus.

When Jesus saw him coming towards him he said:

'Judas, are you going to betray the Son of Man with a kiss?'

The other disciples were wide awake now, and one of them struck the servant of the high priest. But Jesus stopped them from trying to defend him and he said to the guard:

'Do you think I am leading a rebellion? Is that why you have come with your weapons?'

The guard were silent. They did not know what to say to that.

Then the men arrested Jesus and he allowed them to take him away to the house of the high priest.

Peter was the only disciple who followed, but he kept at a distance.

Peter had told Jesus earlier that even if everyone else forsook him he never would. Now was his opportunity to keep his word. Yet later when Jesus needed support from his friends even Peter denied that he knew Jesus.

But he was very sorry about this afterwards.

41

Sentenced to Be Crucified

Jesus was kept all night at the priest's house. All the time his guards mocked him, trying to persuade him to use his miraculous powers.

Very early the next morning he was taken before the Council of Elders, priests and teachers of the law.

'If you are the Christ,' they said, 'tell us.'

'If I tell you,' replied Jesus, 'you won't believe me. But from now on the Son of Man will be seated at the right hand of the mighty God.'

'Are you the Son of God?' they asked.

They were trying to trap Jesus so that they could accuse him of blasphemy. If they could prove that they hoped he would be crucified. But Jesus replied:

'You are right in saying that I am.'

'We don't need to question him further,' they said. 'He has admitted it.'

So they led him off to Pilate.

'Are you the King of the Jews?' asked Pilate.

'Yes, it is as you say,' replied Jesus.

Pilate then told the people who accused Jesus that he could find no fault in him.

'But he is stirring up the people all over the country. He started in Galilee and now he is here with his false teaching.'

When Pilate heard this he thought of a way he could avoid passing sentence. If Jesus came from Galilee he could send him to Herod's court for trial.

But Herod and his soldiers mocked Jesus. They dressed him up in a grand robe and sent him back.

Once more Jesus was before Pilate, who told the chief priests and elders that neither he nor Herod could find any truth in their charges against Jesus.

'He has done nothing to deserve to die,' he said. 'So I will punish him and let him go.'

But the crowd shouted:

'Away with this man. Release Barabbas.'

This was a man who had already been found guilty of murder.

Pilate appealed to them three times to agree to the release of Jesus. But they only shouted louder:

'Crucify him! Crucify him!'

In the end Pilate yielded to their demands. He released the murderer and sentenced Jesus to be crucified.

All this Jesus had to bear before his great suffering and death on the cross. He did God's will to the end of his life on earth.

Jesus Appears to His Followers

Three days after Jesus had been crucified two of the disciples were walking to a village called Emmaus, which is about seven miles from Jerusalem. On the way they talked about all the extraordinary things that had been happening.

As they talked, a stranger joined them.

'What are you talking about so earnestly?' he asked.

'Can't you guess?' asked one of the disciples. 'Don't you know the dreadful thing which has happened in Jerusalem?'

And they told him about Jesus and his trial and crucifixion.

'But,' they added, 'when some of the women went to the tomb where his body lay, it was empty. Jesus wasn't there. So some of the other friends went to see for themselves and they found the women were right. He wasn't there. But even more astonishing, the women said they had a vision of angels who told them he had risen from the dead. Now, how can that be?'

'Why,' said the stranger, 'don't you know all this, about the Christ dying and rising again, is foretold in the Scriptures?'

When they reached Emmaus the disciples invited the stranger to have a meal with them.

And it was only then, when they were at the table, and the stranger gave thanks and broke the bread, that they knew who he was.

The stranger was Jesus.

Later he appeared to the other disciples and then he gave them a command and a promise.

'Stay here until you receive power from above. Then you shall be my witnesses.'

And ever since, many people have done just that—been witnesses for Jesus.